OPEN-TOP BUSES

VERNON SMITH

AMBERLEY

First published 2019

Amberley Publishing
The Hill, Stroud
Gloucestershire, GL5 4EP

www.amberley-books.com

Copyright © Vernon Smith, 2019

The right of Vernon Smith to be identified as
the Author of this work has been asserted in
accordance with the Copyright, Designs and
Patents Act 1988.

ISBN 978 1 4456 9145 9 (print)
ISBN 978 1 4456 9146 6 (ebook)

British Library Cataloguing in Publication Data.
A catalogue record for this book is available from
the British Library.

Origination by Amberley Publishing.
Printed in the UK.

Introduction

Mention open-top buses to most people and it brings up memories of trips to the seaside, where even if the buses weren't travelled on, they were noticed as being something different. However, open-top buses are not restricted to the coast – they are also to be found inland, plying their trade around tourist towns such as Oxford, Bath, Glasgow and of course London, to name a handful.

The earliest horse buses were open-topped, and as this was normal, it would continue onto later trams and motor buses, some of which lasted until the 1940s. As the normal service buses gained roofs, a market developed for buses to take trippers around 'the sights'. Traditionally open-toppers would have been an elderly vehicle, converted to open-top, to spend its last years working for the summer months along the seafront before being stored until the next season. Although this is still true in many cases, purpose-built convertibles have been produced to ensure the most use of the bus by removing the roof and storing it until winter approaches, when the roof would be refitted and the bus used in normal service, Devon General and Southdown being among the best known for this. Another use for them out of season would be as driver trainers, tree loppers (when bus companies did such things) or even to ferry engineers to breakdowns. In many cases an open-topper would carry on in service for many years after the rest of the type has been withdrawn. There are still odd Southdown and Devon General convertibles running, their roofed sisters having come out of mainstream service in 2005. Despite a general decline in seaside open-toppers there has been a small resurgence. Stagecoach in East Kent is one company that had ceased open-top service but have converted modern, low-floor double-deckers for the purpose on the Kent coast; sister company Stagecoach Devon also now has modern, low-floor double-deckers in Torquay. In addition to the planned open-topping of a bus, there are also many instances where buses with roof damage then get converted to open-top. Roof damage normally includes bridge strikes (anything from the front few bays to complete deroofing), and fire damage, both accidental and malicious. These rebuilds are normally done in-house by the operator with varying degrees of success visually. Some vehicles, such as the ex-Southdown and Devon General buses, have been so long lived that they would need a book on their own.

Open-top tourist buses running in popular tourist towns have become more and more common, with many running most of the year using a mixture of open-top, part open-top and closed-top, so covering both their customers and their market share. In the bigger tourist destinations, there is often more than one operator fighting for trade, many using pavement sales staff to drum up as much trade for their bus as possible before the vehicle arrives. London has always been the place for open-top tourist buses, with thousands travelling on the different companies' routes, many running all year round. The London market has seen numerous companies coming, going and merging over the years, resulting in the operations we see today, with many companies now using a mix of older vehicles and brand-new open-toppers. Other towns and cities with sizable open-top services include Bath, Belfast, Dublin, Cambridge, Edinburgh, Glasgow, Oxford and York. Many other towns have more limited services, even a bus operation sponsored by the local council, such as the annual service linking tourist attractions in Chatham, Rochester and Gillingham, which over the years has used a variety of interesting buses!

The story of London sightseeing would need a book in itself, but for the period of this book, a quick overview will suffice. London sightseeing services really started with London Transport's Festival of Britain sightseeing services in 1951, and by the 1980s, London Transport would put out the newest vehicles based at Victoria garage, supplemented by hired-in vehicles which could include ex-London Transport buses, and even ex-Midland Red vehicles. Then, in 1986, the operation was overhauled and re-titled the Original London Transport Sightseeing Tour, using refurbished and open-topped Routemasters. In addition to standard-length Routemasters, ex-Green Line RCLs, ex-British Airways and ex-Northern General versions were used, the sightseeing fleet totalling nearly fifty buses. Originally based at Battersea, the unit moved to Wandsworth in 1988. In the run-up to privatisation London Coaches was formed, now with eighty-five vehicles, before sale to its management in 1992. Competition came in 1984 from London Pride, which merged with Ensign a year later, using ex-London Transport DMS buses, many carrying colourful all-over adverts. Sold by Ensign in 1998, it would be bought back by the company in 2000 and then transformed into a City Sightseeing operation. Another major 1980s operator was Cityrama, running with its familiar blue and white buses, which would also be acquired by Ensign. A small newcomer in 1991 was Big Bus Company, which would grow to be a large company, currently operating in eleven countries, with over 150 vehicles. Other operators came and went, including Blue Triangle, Culturebus, Ebdons, London Tour Co. and London Hop on Hop Off Ltd.

Stratford-upon-Avon-based Guide Friday was established in 1975, and was for many years the dominant sightseeing operator; its green and cream buses could be seen in many towns and cities in both the UK and overseas. After just over twenty-five years, it was bought out by rival City Sightseeing, which is now the world's largest open-top double-deck sightseeing company, with services in over 130 cities worldwide, and a fleet of over 1,000 vehicles. City Sightseeing was originally started by Ensign's Peter Newman, who wished to create a global sightseeing brand – an ambition which he successfully achieved.

Lastly, there are odd open-toppers kept by companies as special events vehicles, which can be used for anything such as a local football team's victory parade, political 'bandwagon', end of term 'prom' vehicles, or simply as an advert for the company at special events, garage open days, fêtes, carnivals, etc.

This book is not meant to be a history of open-toppers, or the companies that use them, but a quick look around the country at the more interesting ones I have photographed. Most of the pictures come from my own collection, and are from the 1980s, 1990s and early 2000s. There is a southern bias, since that is where I am based, and if I have omitted your town or operator, I apologise but I hope it is still of interest!

As in all books, any errors are entirely my own, and should a picture be wrongly credited, please let me know. Among many resources used, the London Omnibus Traction Society, and Rob Sly's Bristol Commercial Vehicles Enthusiasts are two websites that I would highly recommend.

Mention an open-topper to many enthusiasts and the former Southdown Leyland PD3 Queen Marys often comes to mind. Here, 409 DCD, owned by Stagecoach, takes tourists around Eastbourne during the 1995 Rally and Running Day.

Equally well known are the Bristol VRT convertibles. Here, ex-Southdown UWV 604S finishes unloading in Paignton. The bus has been secured in preservation, but sadly only for spares.

New to Northern General, with a spell at City of Oxford before working for Guide Friday Oxford, MPT 314P is seen in a non-PSV role promoting the film *Madagascar*, complete with penguin characters waving from the upper deck as it tours Central London.

Carrying registration 6000 PW, the Virgin Big Brother Diary Room tour bus was found at a hotel just outside of the Sheffield Meadowhall Centre in this August 2008 shot.

BBC World Service ex-London Transport DMS26 is seen parked up in the Aldwych in August 1989.

The direct descendant of London Transport's Round London Tour is the Arriva (later City Sightseeing) Original Tour. A line-up of semi-open-top ex-London Transport Metrobuses are seen in Victoria, led by M533 (GYE 533W).

After the Metrobuses, Alexander-bodied Olympians were converted for use on the Arriva Original London Tour. Here, the former L333 crosses Trafalgar Square.

Like many operators, ex-Hong Kong buses were imported, converted to open/semi-open-top and put to work, the huge upper deck meaning more passengers were carried – vital in the busy summer months. A735 WEV started life with China Motor Bus in 1983 as its ML30, coming to the UK in 2006.

A small group of ex-Arriva London North DAF DB250 Plaxton Presidents were converted to partial open-top for the Original Tour – here, DLP214 (T214 XBV) crosses Trafalgar Square.

Also converted to open-top was former National Express/Wessex 233 (C133 CFB), an MCW Metroliner also seen in Trafalgar Square, with a less than full upper deck.

In 2005 Arriva bought three Volvo B7L with Ayats open-top bodywork for its London tours. LX05 GDZ is seen in Trafalgar Square – after all, what tour bus does not go through here?

Arriva EU05 DVW is seen in March 2007 in full City Sightseeing livery but carrying small 'The Original Tour' stickers over the windscreen and driver's window. It is seen in Trafalgar Square.

Brighton & Hove 022, SPM 22, is seen leaving the seafront after one of the many rallies held there. SPM 22 still exists; having spent a few years in Switzerland, it was last heard of in 2014, being used as a mobile home.

Brighton & Hove 615 was new as a convertible to Southdown, passing to Brighton & Hove in 1986. Passing through various owners, it's currently owned by Seaford & District (shown later in the book). It is seen here in Brighton in July 1994 with its roof on, showing the roof lift rings on the roof edges.

One of a pair of Scania N94UBs, 618 was delivered in 2003 with a convertible East Lancs Omnidekka CO47/32F body and is seen in its original livery, on route 77 to Devils Dyke. Both 617 and 618 passed to Go Ahead North East in 2016.

An earlier pair of convertibles were Dennis Trident 2s with East Lancs Lolyne CO47/31F bodies. 819 *Max Miller* is seen here in a later livery, but still on the 77 to Devils Dyke. Brighton & Hove named their fleet after local people, or people with connections to the area.

New to Crosville, DCA 528X became open-topped in 1991 and carried Arriva corporate blue until withdrawn by the company in 2004. By 2008 it was owned by Classic Bus, Blackpool, and is seen here on the Bournemouth Tour in the same year. (M. Wadman)

New to Cardiff, WTG 360T passed through Bath Bus, Solent Blueline and Southern Vectis before arriving with Classic Bus, Blackpool, to be used on the Bournemouth Tour in 2008. It is now preserved with the Cardiff Transport Preservation Group. (M. Wadman)

Former Leicester Corporation Transport GRY 49D, a Leyland PD3A with Metro-Cammell body, was bought with roof by Castle Point and originally painted in its red/cream livery. Here, it's seen open-topped but still owned by Linkfast Group/Castle Point at the North Weald Rally in 1992.

Bournemouth Yellow Buses 1976 Leyland Fleetline NFX 136P, with Alexander convertible bodywork, is inside Portsmouth naval base during 1991's Navy Days. In addition to the Park and Ride to the base, an internal shuttle/tour was operated, as shown here. This bus was still extant in 2008, when advertised for sale on eBay.

Naturally, Blackpool has open-toppers. This is Blackpool Transport's 818, an ex-London Olympian (D218 FYM), seen loading beside the Tower in 2009. Blackpool obtained seven of these from Ensign between 2006 and 2008. Withdrawal for 818 for scrap came in 2012.

Seen rounding Parliament Square in August 1988 is Blue Triangle's ex-Northern General Routemaster FPT 588C, carrying fleet number RMO2118. After a spell with Big Bus, this bus is believed to be on Malta.

A more recent member of the Blue Triangle fleet is Leyland Titan T512, seen rounding Trafalgar Square in 2006. Converted after an upper deck fire, this former Stagecoach East London bus had a spell with Stagecoach Cumbria, which sold it to Blue Triangle in 2005. Upon sale of Blue Triangle to Go Ahead, T512 passed on to Roger Wright's London Bus Company.

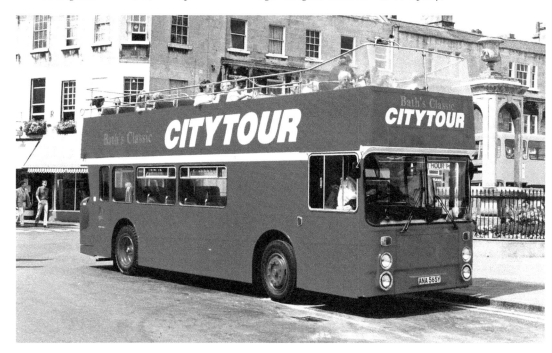

Ryan Tours' Bath City Tour used this 1982 ex-Greater Manchester Leyland Atlantean with Northern Counties body, ANA 565Y, seen in August 1998. (M. Wadman)

Also used by Ryan's on their Bath tour was ex-Southdown VRT TNJ 996S. Twin-door open-tops are not common, but this one managed to retain its centre doors during its service life. Acquired in 1990, it left the Ryan fleet in 2006. (M. Wadman)

New to Southdown, UWV 619S passed through Brighton & Hove before joining Ryan's in 1999. Leaving the fleet in 2007, it was sold via a dealer to a company in Spain. Here, UWV 619S is caught at speed on the A38 in Devon, heading to Plymouth to catch its ferry from Plymouth's Millbay Docks.

The Bristol City Guided Tour's LDX 75G, an ex-Ipswich Atlantean with ECW bodywork, which had been part of a pair operated by Eastbourne Buses. Compare this 1998 picture with a view later in the book working in Eastbourne. (M. Wadman)

A former Bristol Omnibus Lodekka, 841 SHW was rebuilt to open-top in 1976, leaving Bristol Omnibus Co. in 1982. It joined the West of England Transport Collection and is seen here in 1998 on loan to Warwick Hulme (with maintenance support from Crown Coaches and A-Bus) on the Bristol Tour. After four years on this, it was loaned to Mac Tours, Edinburgh, for three years. (M. Wadman)

Big Bus is a now a worldwide operator but started in 1991 with a mere four buses. Here, PFN 853, a former East Kent AEC Regent V, passes Trafalgar Square. It is by now used for information and ticket sales.

Also in use for ticket sales and information at Victoria in 2004 is XMD 47A (formerly KCH 106), an ex-Trent PD2/12 with Metro-Cammell bodywork.

Sitting beside Victoria station in April 2004 is DMS1958, clearly in use as an information point judging from the number of leaflets and the map in the windscreen.

In addition to the standard DMS, Big Bus also has the B20 version, as seen with DMS2365, also caught parked up near Victoria.

Ex-London Titans followed the DMSs into the fleet. In August 2006 canvas-roofed convertible T722 is seen crossing Trafalgar Square, being pursued by a Mercedes-Benz bendy bus on the 12.

G96 SGD is one of several ex-Hong Kong/Chinese buses to have entered the Big Bus fleet and is seen near Victoria, showing its huge length off.

At the same location in July 2006, Big Bus partial open-top Titan T1024 shows off its neat conversion to single-door.

Queueing at Trafalgar Square is Big Bus open-top, two-door Titan MB 5919 (T919).

Heading across Trafalgar Square is Big Bus Dennis Condor/Duple Metsec partial open-top B14 BUS.

Cityrama is best known for blue and white DMS buses, but here is Cityrama RCH 515F, a former Trent 1968 Daimler Fleetline, converted to partial open-top, in an eye-catching livery for Thai Air.

Making its way around Aldwych in June 1988 is Cityrama 29, ex-London Buses DMS2029. Like many fleets, Cityrama had examples of open, part-open, and enclosed buses in its fleet.

In 1986 Trafalgar Square still had buses passing on all four sides. Here, Cityrama DMS124 and 2159 are double-parked, with a London Sightseeing Tours DMS and Greenline AN class Atlantean behind.

Here we see part-open-top RCH 515F again, now speeding around Aldwych in fleet livery with a Metrobus on the 11 in hot pursuit.

Another unusual vehicle among the DMSs was XWX 56G, one of a pair of former West Yorkshire Bristol VRTs. New to West Yorkshire in February 1969, XWX 56G was scrapped in 1991.

Following a diversion off Fleet Street, fully open-topped Cityrama DMS1623 takes its passengers past the delights of Holborn Viaduct (behind the camera).

Yet another oddity in Cityrama's fleet was GWA 825N, a former South Yorkshire PTE Daimler Fleetline, new in April 1975.

Closed-top JWF 47W, a Leyland Atlantean/Roe, was new to Cityrama/Limebourne and was added on to the end of an order for West Yorkshire PTE. Later, JWF 47W operated for Eastbourne Buses, Geoff Amos and City Central, Hull.

Back to Bath now, and Badgerline 8608. New as a convertible to Hants & Dorset in 1977, it moved to Southern Vectis in 1979, before joining Bristol Omnibus in 1983 and then staying with Badgerline and its successor First Group companies until it was retired in 2005 for preservation. (M. Wadman)

Badgerline's ex-Maidstone & District Atlantean 612 UKM is seen in 1992 – complete with badger holding bucket and spade. After Badgerline, and a spell at Torquay, it moved north to Hall of Kennoway. (M. Wadman)

Seen a year later in 1993 is Badgerline's ex-Bristol open-top VRT 8619 (JHW 114P). New to Bristol in 1976, it was converted to open-top in 1985, staying with First until 2000. It was altered to offside entrance and exported to Canada in October 2000. (M. Wadman)

Former Devon General VDV 818, a 1957 AEC Regent V, was often used to link the South Devon Railway with nearby Buckfastleigh town – a duty since often shared with a Routemaster, RM1872. VDV 818 is part of the West of England Transport Collection and was seen at Buckfastleigh in 2004.

Devon General is well-known for running open-top buses. Here, the then current fleet of convertible VRTs is seen parked up in Exmouth bus station on 1 October 1990. From left to right: VDV140/139/135S, named *Invincible*, *Ark Royal* and *Exeter* respectively.

Parked against the back wall, but in full view of the bus station, were all three of Devon General's convertible VRT roofs, stacked on what seems to be an old bus chassis.

Eastbourne ran two ex-Ipswich open-top Atlanteans with ECW bodies, painted cream and red or blue – the former, LDX 75G, *Eastbourne Queen*, is seen leaving Eastbourne en route to Beachy Head.

Although not a PSV, a well-known open-top resident at East Kent's Herne Bay garage was tree lopper MFN 939F, a 1967 AEC Regent V. It is seen in its usual position beside the garage in 1984.

A trip to see the East Kent open-top VRTs turned to disaster as they were all tucked up in Westwood garage! However, all was not lost as a friendly inspector allowed me to roam around inside the garage. Bristol VRT 7616 (UWV 616S) is seen at the head of the line.

London Hop on Hop Off LUF 132F, new as Brighton Corporation 32 and converted to open-top while in Brighton. This Leyland PD3/4 is seen at Marble Arch in November 1994. (M. Wadman)

London Hop On Hop Off BHM288, an ex-Southdown Queen Mary PD3 (410 DCD), seen at Marble Arch in November 1994. It is now preserved in full Southdown traditional green and cream livery. (M. Wadman)

Used by Ensign in the 1980s, PHJ 351 was a former Southend Corporation Leyland PD3 with Massey body. Converted by that operator in 1970/1, this bus was later exported to Germany. It is seen at the Plumstead Garage Open Day in June 1983.

First Devon & Cornwall 39901, a former Grampian Leyland Atlantean AN68 with Alexander body, swings into Penzance's bus station on 18 July 2006.

First Devon & Cornwall 39902, another converted Atlantean, is also seen turning at Penzance bus station in July 2006, still with one full bay on the upper deck.

First Devon & Cornwall 39902 is seen later in 2006 but has now had the remaining front bay removed and replaced with lower windows, and handrails have been added along the side bodywork. It is seen parked in Plymouth's Bretonside bus station in October 2006.

New to Bristol Omnibus, 39908 was converted to open-top by Hants & Dorset in 1985. Passing to First Devon & Cornwall in 2005, it stands at Penzance bus station with route and destination details on the paper notice in front of the driver (300 Penzance). It passed to Chepstow Classic Bus in 2005 and stayed there until moving into preservation in 2011.

Delivered as a convertible in 1978, 1003 stayed with Western National/First Devon & Cornwall for its entire life until it was withdrawn in 2007, when it was preserved in GWR colours. It was seen here on Plymouth Hoe for the 2009 Plymouth Rally.

Seen at the Plymouth Hoe 2007 Rally, this is 30001, a VRT2 which started out with PMT and was converted to permanent open-top in 1990. A move west to First Devon & Cornwall came in 2003 and it stayed there until 2008, when it joined the ranks of preserved VRTs.

First Devon & Cornwall Olympian 34750 turns in Penzance bus station in July 2008. Delivered as a standard closed-top vehicle, 34750 did not last long as an open-topper, being replaced by Volvo Citybuses.

Seen stored at Winkleigh, Devon, in 2007, these are First Olympians 39913 and 34750, both of which only served for a couple of seasons before withdrawal. 39913 is currently preserved.

Seen in typical British weather, 30020 (RTH 931S) was new to South Wales in 1977, staying until 1991 when it joined Badgerline. Staying with various western First Group companies, it reached First Devon & Cornwall in 2004, staying until 2008, when it left for preservation in Wales.

Seen making its way up onto Plymouth Hoe is 38000 (D700 GHY), a Volvo B10M Citybus with Alexander RV bodywork new to Badgerline.

Seen on Plymouth Hoe picking up passengers while attending the Plymouth Hoe Rally and Running Day 2008, D706 GHY is still in service. It is no longer owned by First but was hired to Mendip Mule Motorbus in 2018.

A Frames Rickards ex-Lancaster City Council Leyland Atlantean with MCW bodywork, DBA 230C is seen rounding the Aldwych during the 1980s.

Guide Friday was one of the largest sightseeing bus companies before being taken over by City Sightseeing, with tours all over the UK. Seen leaving Plymouth's Bretonside bus station in 1990 is former Edinburgh Atlantean OSF 928M.

Seen on Plymouth Hoe in 1990 is ex-Nottingham BVT 657T. Guide Friday buses were allowed to drive onto the Hoe as part of the tour – something that has long since stopped, with buses keeping to the roads along the front of the Hoe.

Guide Friday ETO 178L is seen picking up in Oxford in July 1991. Delivered new to Nottingham City Transport in 1973 as its 178, this Fleetline has Willowbrook bodywork to standard Nottingham style.

Also working the Oxford Tour is ex-Eastbourne Leyland Atlantean KHC 817K with East Lancs bodywork. The pictures on the buses depicting local tourist features were a feature of the Guide Friday livery.

Hastings now, where the original low height VRT was joined under Stagecoach by this former Southdown VRT convertible, UWV 623S, seen on Hastings seafront in 1995. Withdrawn in 1999, the bus is currently owned by Romer of Bournemouth.

Lettered for the Bournemouth tour, this is WOW 529J – a former Southampton Corporation Leyland Atlantean PDR1A with East Lancs bodywork, which had also worked the Southampton tour before preservation in this livery.

Passing through Brighton in July 1994, this is GYS 896D, a former Glasgow Leyland Atlantean PDR1/1 which has been reconverted to closed-top and is now preserved as part of the Glasgow Vintage Vehicle Trust.

This former Portsmouth Corporation 1966 Leyland Atlantean, ERV 254D, is seen on the Brighton tour in July 1994. The bus had also worked in London tours, in both covered and open-top form.

This former Plymouth Citybus Atlantean is seen back in Plymouth, but still showing details for the Newport tour, with fleet number 8154 showing alongside its Plymouth number. The railway shown over the front door is the Great Central Railway. This bus is also now preserved.

Seen on the Cambridge tour is CWF 736T, an ex-South Yorkshire twin-door Atlantean which had also served on the Medway tour in Kent.

The Oxford tour had OTO 549M on it in 2004, with the front panel showing the takeover of Guide Friday by City Sightseeing. This former Nottingham Fleetline, owned by Tappins, would soon receive full City Sightseeing livery.

To celebrate Plymouth Argyle's promotion to Division Two in 2004, the team toured Plymouth on three Plymouth Citybus open-top Atlanteans. With a suitably large flag, ODV 203V heads the convoy beside the Civic Centre.

Here is Plymouth Citybus Atlantean 161 showing off its two-door layout – by now, the open-tops were the only two-door buses left in the fleet. It is also seen parked up beside the Civic Centre in May 2004.

Seen in Brighton is ex-Nottingham UTV 215S. This Daimler Fleetline is in the generic livery for the 'city tour' complete with two pictures of Guide Friday buses on the side, to enable it to cover anywhere in the Guide Friday empire.

Harris Bus had this ex-Southdown Queen Mary, BUF 426C, in its fleet. This bus has also joined the ranks of preserved Queen Marys, restored to Southdown livery.

One of Devon General's Sea Dog Leyland Atlanteans, preserved 931 GTA is seen in 2008 while reversing into position at the Westpoint, Exeter, rally.

Seen parked at the Plumstead Garage Open Day is DMO3, one of a number of ex-Bournemouth Daimler Fleetlines with convertible bodywork by Weymann. New in 1965, LT acquired them in 1977, basing them at Stockwell for London sightseeing duties, both with and without their roofs.

Summercourt Travel UWV 613S waits time in Newquay. It was refitted with a removable roof and exported to Spain in 2008. Starting out with Southdown, it then worked for various companies, including East Kent, Bluebird and Chepstow Classic Buses.

People's Provincial 592 (NFX 131P), an ex-Bournemouth convertible Daimler Fleetline with Alexander bodywork, is seen in Portsmouth Harbour on the 114 to Eastney.

Kentish Bus converted two early Atlanteans to open-top. Here, 901 is seen ensuring everyone knew who was sponsoring the 1993 Sevenoaks Running Day.

Award-winning Kent coach company the Kings Ferry has operated various open-tops over the years. Here, their former Southdown PD3 is seen parked at Chatham Historic Dockyard. Ex-Southdown PRX 207B is now preserved with its original registration, 410 DCD, in traditional Southdown colours.

For the 2006 Summer Medway Towns Tour, Kings Ferry was using AFX 184X, a Willowbrook-bodied Atlantean AN68B/1R which had seen service with Stotts of Oldham, Maghull Coaches and Merseyside PTE.

The 2007 Summer Medway Tour featured ex-London DMS1958, seen approaching the Rochester stop. New to London Transport, KUC 958P had also worked with Big Bus Tours in London.

New to Crosville, Lodekka 882 VFM was used to promote Lloyd Williams estate agents. After rebranding to Mullocks Wells estate agents, the bus was finally exported to Hong Kong, but it may now be in Japan. It is seen at the 1990 North Weald Rally.

Open-top single-deckers are unusual but here we see ex-Maidstone & District HKL 819 arriving at the 2007 Hastings Rally. It is one of three AEC Regals converted in 1957 for use in Hastings (and elsewhere if required), all three of which have managed to survive into preservation.

York railway station is the setting for City Sightseeing ex-London Metrobus GYE 603W, working for Top Line Travel in 2006.

Still at York station, we find Top Line Travel LBO 501X, with the guide clearly earning his money. New to Cardiff City Transport, LBO 501X is a Leyland Olympian with East Lancs bodywork. Note the Guide Friday branding under the front windows.

Former London Buses M115 (new in 1979) is also working for Top Line Travel, York.

Working the Newcastle Red Route in July 2006, this is former London BYX 241V, now with Stagecoach Busways but still carrying the Inverness Sightseeing livery from its previous allocation (the Inverness branding was above the staircase thistle).

Complete with an offside door, M647 RCP, a DAF DB250 with Northern Counties bodywork, passes through Brighton. In closed-top form, it had previously operated for Capital Citybus, and Blue Bus, Horwich,

Brighton & Hove 781, R881 HCD, a Scania with East Lancs bodywork, was displayed at the 2010 Cobham Bus Rally carrying the name *Anne of Cleeves* and clear Brighton tour branding.

Chester City Transport 996, a 1980 Leyland Fleetline with Northern Counties body. Previously in Guide Friday green, 996 now sports full City Sightseeing livery.

Also in Chester, but in 2008, we find an ex-London Olympian, D183 FYM, now with First Potteries as its 39933; First had three Olympians for the Chester tour. 39933 was new to London Buses as its L183 in 1986 and has since been scrapped.

Back to the tourist hotspot of Oxford. Here, PO55 NXU, a Tappins Volvo B7TL with an East Lancs Myllennium Vyking part-open-top body, waits time before the next tour.

This is Tappins ex-Plymouth City Transport GJZ 9574 (STK 124T), a Leyland AN68/1R with Roe dual-door bodywork now converted to single-door.

Tappins ex-Nottingham Daimler Fleetline GJZ 9576 works the Oxford tour in 2006. It was new in 1977 to Nottingham City Transport as its 217, before open-topping with Guide Friday. After repainting in City Sightseeing red, the bus was scrapped in 2007.

EWF 453V, an ex-South Yorkshire PTE Metrobus, is seen in Ramsgate. Previously with Grey Green (with roof), London Pride and the Cambridge Tour, it later worked the Colchester tour for Talisman.

Tappins 51 (MUI 7851), formerly 90-D-1013, an ex-Dublin Bus Olympian with Alexander (Belfast) bodywork, cruises through Oxford complete with small Guide Friday stickers on the front and sides.

Ex-London Central Volvo Olympian N548 LHG was being used on the Beachy Head–Eastbourne service in 2008. It has also been used on the Bath and Cardiff tours. Its Northern Counties body still has two doors from its London days.

Crossing Trafalgar Square is Arriva Olympian J319 BSH (DA319) with Alexander part-open-top bodywork. New to London Buses Leaside, this bus later worked with Discover Dorset, Bournemouth, complete with London graphics.

Displayed at the 2004 North Weald Rally, this is Guide Friday E767 LBT, an ex-South Yorkshire bus in full City Sightseeing Windsor livery. It would later be exported to Cyprus around 2010.

Awaiting passengers on the Bristol tour is Rubicon Travel's T75 KLD, a former Metroline Dennis Trident with Alexander ALX400 bodywork. (M. Wadman)

Ensignbus ex-London DMS33, an early version with the close together headlights, is exhibited at the 2003 North Weald Rally. This bus also has the early style conversion to single-door, with the smaller window replacing the centre door.

During the 1980s and 1990s, DMSs could always be found sightseeing in London. Here, Maxell-liveried DMS840 passes Holborn Viaduct station (behind the camera) while on diversion from its normal route.

Ensign's former London Transport DMS159 rounds the Aldwych sporting a LBC Radio advert in June 1987. Previously the bus had worked for Ebdons Tours, both with and without its roof.

One of the more striking liveries was for 7-UP on DMS165, which is also seen in the Aldwych. This 1971 DMS was later exported to Gray Line, Toronto.

Beauty is in the eye... Leaving the Aldwych is London Pride DMS287, complete with dragons! New to London Transport, this vehicle had also been with Ebdons Tours.

Slightly more unusual was PUF 716M, an ex-Southdown 1973 Atlantean with Park Royal body, which had also worked for Ribble before becoming an open-topper.

Showing a different LBC Radio advert is DMS813, which also worked London tours for Ebdon's Coaches, Sidcup.

Possibly the most eye-catching of the Ensign/London Pride DMSs was DMS586, whose XXXX lager advert also had bull bars and a 'ram's head' on the front dash.

Seen stored in the Dartford garage of Kentish Bus are a large number of Ensign/London Pride DMSs, with DMS159 and DMS158 standing side-by-side.

Seen parked up opposite my old employer, Beatties of London Ltd, is DMS33, which we saw earlier in the book in Ensign blue and cream. New in 1970, it's now back in red and cream and it is in the Ensign Heritage fleet.

As we have seen before, more upper deck seats are always needed, so former Shamrock & Rambler A112 KFX, an MCW Metroliner double-deck coach, was converted to open-top – a far cry from its days as a National Express front-line vehicle.

Rounding the Aldwych in May 1990 is ex-Portsmouth MCW/Atlantean ERV 247D, now in the service of London Sightseeing Tours Limited. When previously owned by Maybury, this bus had been hired to LT, with roof, for use on the London Sightseeing Tour.

Passing through Parliament Square in 1988 is ex-London Transport DMS141, which has retained its centre exit doors. The bus would later be exported to the US.

Seen a little off route, former London DMS372 is passing Red Lion Square. London Sightseeing named their buses, this one being named *Carol*. After the 1993 season it would be exported to Apple Tours, New York.

London Sightseeing's DMS2132 not only carried the name *Nellie*, but also this striking advert for the London Dungeon. It is seen in the Aldwych, followed by another London Sightseeing DMS, both with good loads of tourists onboard.

Ex-United OCS 590H, a Bristol VRT/SL6G/ECW which was new to Western SMT in November 1969, rounds the Aldwych while working for the London Tour Co. in May 1989.

Seen in the Aldwych again is London Tour Co. PBC 102G, an ex-Leicester City Transport Leyland Atlantean PDR1A/1 with ECW bodywork, complete with happy face!

Parked up in London's Russell Square is JK 5605, in promotional livery for Tobacco Dock. New to Eastbourne Corporation in 1936/7, it was open-topped in 1952, leaving Eastbourne in 1963. This bus is currently preserved in Eastbourne colours.

Among the buses attending Showbus at Woburn Abbey in 1989 was RM1403, which had been converted to open-top by Benskins Brewery – hence the Castlemaine XXXX (an Australian beer) destination blind.

On the long-gone Piccadilly Circus bus stand in June 1983 is Obsolete Fleet's OM1, a former Midland Red D9, and one of seven buses converted to open-top, along with a handful which retained their roofs. Obsolete Fleet ceased operations later in 1983.

Other buses hired to LT for use on the Round London Sightseeing Tour (RLST) at this time was London Country Leyland Atlantean AN110, in full London red livery. It is seen in Victoria in June 1983.

London Transport had also traditionally used its newest buses on the RLST. Seen here inside Gillingham Street (Victoria) garage, in June 1986, is Leyland B20 DMS DM2585.

London Transport gave the RLST a major facelift, using recently redundant Routemasters, mainly converted to open-top, Here, RM562 turns right into Whitehall – note the subtle renaming to the Original London Transport Sightseeing Tour (OLTST) and the wider (RCL style) front blind box.

Also used on the OLTST were both RCL and RMA type Routemasters. Rounding the Aldwych in June 1989 is RCL2245 – perhaps rain was forecast later that day. The platform doors were reinstated for London sightseeing duties.

RM1783 takes a good load around the Aldwych, in immaculate condition and retaining a full drop air intake under the destination blinds.

An oddity in the fleet was RMF2793, which was one of the Routemasters supplied new to Northern General. Unlike most open-top conversions, it has the RMC-style blinds with a smaller via blind. EUP 406B is seen at my favourite location – Aldwych.

To increase seating capacity, a small number of standard Routemasters were extended using an additional bay, taken from scrap vehicles. The extended vehicles became ERMs, as shown by ERM242 in August 1990, complete with additional advertising.

Upon privatisation, London Coaches (which was operating the OLTST) had to remove the London Transport part of the name, becoming the Original London Sightseeing Tour (OLST). Seen at 1997's North Weald Rally, this is convertible RCL2220 in a striking advert for the Tower of London.

Arriva London has kept a small heritage fleet of Routemasters, including RMC1464, seen here arriving at the Stokes Bay Rally, complete with advertising for the Arriva Heritage fleet.

Captured at the 2010 Cobham Rally is X172 FBB, a former East Thames Buses Volvo B7TL with Plaxton President bodywork that passed to London Central, who had last used it as a training bus. It is now part of London Bus Services, Victoria Street, London SW1.

London Northern M804 is displayed at the 1993 North Weald Rally. M804 had been part of the batch delivered to Sidcup garage for comparative tests against Titans and DMSs. Now converted to single-door, it became London Northern's special events vehicle.

Leyland B20 DM2291 was used for one summer season on the Medway Towns Tour and was given M&D fleet number 5666 for its stay. New in 1977, it was converted to open-top around 1986 and used by London Northern as the Lea Valley leisure bus and for private hires. It would finally be scrapped in 2009.

London General M241 was also used by Maidstone & District on the Medway tour, and is seen here arriving at Chatham station. New in 1980 and used by London General as a special events and private hire vehicle, it would go on to work with City Sightseeing.

Prior to the need to hire in open-tops, Maidstone & District kept this 1973 Atlantean with MCW bodywork, FKM 706L, as their special events bus. After a spell in South Devon, this bus was preserved.

Hastings & District used a low height Bristol VR Series 2 for their tour bus. HKE 690L is seen in Hastings in 1991 and would lose this livery later on, being replaced with Guide Friday green and cream. After spells with Chepstow Classic Buses and a spell in preservation, HKR 690L joined Seaford & District, with whom it still works.

A brief entrant into the Oxford tour market was Oxford Full Circle. Here we see A722 UOE, a former West Midlands Mk 2 Metrobus, new in 1984. After a spell with Guide Friday, City Sightseeing and some non-PSV work, it was scrapped in 2009.

Also in the Full Circle fleet was WTS 272T, an ex-Travel Dundee Volvo Ailsa with Alexander bodywork. Full Circle was acquired by City Sightseeing in February 2005.

The Oxford Classic Tour was operated jointly by Tappins and Lothian Buses. Here, panoramic-windowed Leyland Atlantean BFS 14L awaits more passengers.

Plymouth Citybus kept this Leyland Titan PD2/12/MCW open-topper, new to Plymouth in September 1956. Named *Sir Francis Drake* upon conversion to open-top, this bus has been the Citybus events vehicle for many years. Seen in 2008, *Sir Francis Drake* has since been repainted cream.

Replacements for Plymouth's PD2s came from the Atlantean fleet, as shown by 458 (WJY 758, *Plymouth Adventurer*), seen by the Hoe on a bright summer's day. After spells in Scarborough, York and the Keighley Bus Museum, the bus is now preserved.

After years at the Keighley Bus museum, WYJ 758 is now preserved back in the South West. Still carrying its former owner's colours, it's seen at the Plymouth Hoe Rally.

River Link's route 100 was a vital part of River Link's 'Round Robin' train, boat and bus ride. Here, UWV 604S is seen in Paignton in July 2006. New to Southdown as a convertible, it also worked for Hampshire Bus, Bay Line and Devon General. It has been preserved as a source of spares.

New to Southdown in 1978, UWV 614S also worked for Bayline before spending sixteen years with Dart Pleasure Craft (River Link). An open-top run through the Devon fields on a VRT on a summer evening was not to be missed. Seen leaving Paignton bus station in 2004, this bus is now preserved.

Delivered to Crosville and spending time there with Midland Red and Crosville Wales, WTU 467W was open-topped in 1995 and worked with River Link until preservation called in 2016. River Link operated around six VRTs before moving onto ex-Plymouth Atlanteans and Darts, and currently use low-floor Volvo B7TL/Plaxton Presidents new to London General.

Delivered to Portsmouth Corporation, LRV 992 is seen posed at the 1990 North Weald Rally. Retained by Stagecoach and transferred to Stagecoach South West for special events, it is currently painted in Devon General colours.

Attending the 2009 North Weald Rally is Guernseybus-liveried former London Transport RT2494, which is now preserved and a regular at rallies.

Parked in Brighton's Pool Valley bus station is Southdown's SPM 21, a Bristol Lodekka FS6B with convertible bodywork. New in 1960 to Brighton, Hove & District, SPM 21 survived until 1991, when the bus was exported to Switzerland, where it was used as a mobile home.

Shown at the 1983 Bluebell Railway Bus Rally, this is Southdown Bristol Lodekka convertible RPN 11, which was withdrawn and exported from the UK in 1990. Note the 'cheaper with Beeper' advert – a very popular advertising campaign of the time.

One of the iconic Southdown PD3/4s, 410 DCD has been restored to full Southdown colours after a spell with Ensign/London Pride (shown earlier in the book). It also regained its original registration number, having been DHJ 301B (and BHM 288 and PRX 207B) for a while.

A much-travelled former Southdown VRT, UWV 615S is seen loading in Eastbourne while working for Village Coaches. Having been preserved twice, this bus is once again preserved in Devon, with a roof once more.

As is well known, Southend has a very long pier, and has had open-top services running underneath it for many years. Attending the Croydon depot open day in 1983 was Fleetline 915, in a striking livery for the Essex Sunday Saver ticket. Note the RM just behind.

South Midland had a small fleet of mainly DMSs for sightseeing work in Oxford and Blenheim. Here, ex-LT DMS1840 turns in Salters Boat Yard, where passengers could leave/join Salter Bros sightseeing boats on the River Thames.

Nicely parked up at Blenheim Palace, in full tour livery, is ex-LT DM1121. South Midland had four DMSs and a Bristol VRT. DM1121 also worked in London and Bath as a sightseer.

Back to the Salter Bros boatyard, and DMS886 is seen unloading by the slipway. To access this point tour buses had to pass alongside the caravan and camping part of the often muddy site.

Standing outside of Stagecoach's Romford garage during the 2003 open day is JAH 552D. Part of the initial Cambus fleet, it would work under the Viscount and Premier liveries before being repainted into Stagecoach national colours, and is now part of the Stagecoach Heritage fleet.

Another of the Southdown VRT convertibles, UWV 621S is seen working for Stagecoach South Coast Buses at the Eastbourne station stop in May 1995 before heading to Beachy Head. Used in non-PSV roles after 1999, the scrapyard beckoned in about 2013.

Even the VRTs had to retire, so Stagecoach converted several ex-London Scania N113s to open-top – most of which could be reroofed if needed. J829 HMC was a permanent open-topper, and is seen in the Paignton one-way system, on the 200 to Totnes via the excellent Paignton Zoo.

Seen loading in Torquay in August 2004 is Stagecoach J827 HMC (15327), also on the 200 but this time showing a full set of via points. This bus was another permanent open-topper and was withdrawn in 2011.

Starting life with Grimsby Cleethorpes Transport (GCT), this is MBE 613R, a Leyland Fleetline with Roe dual-door bodywork which was converted to open-top in 1994. Seen arriving at the Heaton Park 2006 Rally, the bus has since been preserved and repainted into full GCT livery.

Stagecoach East Kent 17528, an ex-London Transbus ALX400 normally found on route 69 from Ramsgate to Broadstairs, is seen loading at 2018's Herne Bay Rally. A similar vehicle is the spare, but in a simplified livery.

Stagecoach entered the London sightseeing market in 2018, using former London ALX400s again, under the Megasightseeing brand. Here, 18475 *King Henry VIII* is displayed at the 2018 South East Bus Festival, in Detling, Kent.

New to Southend Transport, JTD 395P is seen on Torquay seafront while working with Merrivale Ltd and taking visitors to Babbacombe Model Village. New in 1976, this bus is preserved at the Castle Point Transport Museum, Canvey Island.

Having just arrived in Poole bus station in this May 2004 view, this is Leyland Olympian A174 VFM. New to Crosville, it later became a tree cutter with Southern Vectis, in the same livery but with a yellow front.

A bus with a long history, CJH 119V started life with Alder Valley and was open-topped in 1999, ending up with Western Greyhound in 2003. Staying with Western Greyhound for five years, it has since been fitted with an offside door and is currently with a Warrington dealer, painted red.

This former West Yorkshire PTE Olympian with Roe bodywork is seen on the Whitby Town Tour, working for Coastal & Country Coaches. Prior to this UWW 2X had worked in Chester for Chester City Transport.

Immaculate ex-London Buses Titan T1092 is seen in York with York Pullman, making a sharp right turn by the city wall. Having also worked for Stagecoach, T1092 was exported to the US.

Seen at the same location is York Pullman's Routemaster RM787, carrying registration 792 UXA, which came from Quantock Heritage Coaches, Taunton, in whose livery it worked.

G. H. Watts of Leicester has ex-Lothian Regional Transport DSX 87L (BFS44L), a Leyland Atlantean AN68/1R with Alexander AL bodywork which came from Guide Friday.

Arriving at the 1992 Showbus Rally is Whippet's Metropolitan WKH 426S. New in 1978 to Hull City Transport, it has been stored for the past few years and is believed to currently be with Ensign.

For 1997, McNaughton (Rochester Tours) used C537 TJF on tours of Rochester, Kent. It was formerly a standard sixteen-seat minibus with Midland Fox, Leicester.

Ex-Tayside Volvo B10M G91 PES has been converted to a theatre bus for IOU Theatre, Halifax. It can work in two ways – either the audience sits in the bus to watch the show or vice versa. Here, it's in the car park of B&Q, Eltham, south-east London, despite it apparently being based at the First depot in Halifax. (K. Trump)

Found in use as a billboard and shop just outside of Ruxley Nurseries, this is Y191 NLK, a former Metroline Volvo B7TL with Plaxton bodywork. After a spell with London City Tour, it was painted green before taking up residence at the front of the nursery in Kent. (K. Hollands)

Leisurelink (Abacus) had 928 GTA, a former Devon General Seadog Atlantean, for a while, and used it often on the Surrey Hills leisure bus. It is seen here at the 1995 Southsea Rally.

Leisurelink also had ex-Southern Vectis Lodekka MDL 954, which was converted to open-top around 1973. Although preserved, the bus has been loaned to various operators, including Abacus, for the 1992–3 Surrey Hills network. It was photographed at the Croydon Garage Open Day in June 1992.